BOX TURTLES

WEIRD PETS

Lynn M. Stone

Rourke Publishing LLC
Vero Beach, Florida 32964

www.rourkepublishing.com

PHOTO CREDITS:
All photos © Lynn M. Stone

EDITORIAL SERVICES:
Pamela Schroeder

Library of Congress Cataloging-in-Publication Data

Stone, Lynn M.
    Box Turtles / Lynn M. Stone
        p. cm—(Weird Pets)
    ISBN 1-58952-037-8
    1.Box turtles as pets—Juvenile literature [1. Box turtles. 2. Turtles
    as pets. 3. Pets.] I. Title.

SF459.T8 S78 2001
639.3'925—dc21   00-054286

Printed in the USA

TABLE OF CONTENTS

BOX TURTLES

Box turtles are unusual pets and unusual turtles. They're not like other turtles. They can close themselves up, like a box.

Box turtles and most other turtles are wrapped in a bone-hard shell. The top of the shell is called the **carapace**. The bottom is the **plastron**. A turtle pulls its head inside the shell to protect itself.

A shy box turtle peeks out from under its shell.

The box turtle's shell is special. The plastron has a hinge toward the front. The hinge snaps shut like a trap door. A box turtle closes in its head and front feet at one end. It closes up its tail and hind feet at the other end.

Box turtles are small and often colorful. They have a high, rounded shell. Sometimes the shell has bright, yellow markings almost like zebra stripes.

This is the box turtle's underside, or plastron, closed tightly.

Different kinds of box turtles live all over the United States and in parts of Mexico. They don't live in ponds or lakes. They live in the deserts and prairies of the Midwest and West. They live in the moist woodlands of the South and East.

Box turtles are not fussy eaters. They are true **omnivores**. They eat plant and animal food. A box turtle may eat raspberries one day and earthworms the next. People who keep box turtles as pets need to be sure to mix their turtles' diet.

The eastern box turtle is the most colorful type of American box turtle.

Box turtles have become hard to find in many places. Cars crush thousands of them on roads. People pick up thousands more. New buildings and roads have taken over box turtle **habitats**, or homes.

Often a dull color, three-toed box turtles live in the south central United States.

11

Pet box turtles need to be protected from dogs and raccoons.

Captive box turtles need a place to eat, and good owners add vitamins to turtle foods.

Box turtles are most often seen after late spring rains. They move about less in the summer and early fall. Box turtles in cold areas **hibernate** in winter. Hibernation is a deep sleep. A hibernating turtle lives off its stored body fat. To hibernate, the turtle digs into the ground. It must dig deep enough to stay below where the ground will freeze.

Pet box turtles in the North get ready for five months of hibernation in loose soil and wood chips.

BOX TURTLES: PET FRIENDLY?

Box turtles are tough but gentle animals. They eat well in **captivity**, and they're fun to watch when they're active.

However, box turtles are wild animals. Some states have laws against keeping wild animals.

Box turtles may carry dangerous germs. Anyone who handles turtles should wash with strong soap.

16

In some states, including Connecticut, it is illegal to take a box turtle from its wild habitat.

CARING FOR BOX TURTLES

Anyone who wants to keep a box turtle should first learn about the turtle's needs. Find books about box turtle care and visit on-line sites. Ask questions of **reptile** club members or talk to box turtle owners.

The best place to keep a box turtle is outdoors. The turtle's pen should be roomy and well built. The turtle needs a shallow water dish for soaking. A child's swimming pool is not good. The pool sides are too high. A turtle can drown if it cannot climb out of the water.

The sides of the pen should be wood, brick, or plastic. They should go underground, too. Box turtles can dig out of the pen if the sides aren't deep enough.

A box turtle must be protected from dogs and raccoons. Chicken wire above the pen will help keep the turtles safe.

The perfect box turtle home has sunshine, shade, water, loose soil, and natural foods.

FINDING A BOX TURTLE

Many pet box turtles are taken from the wild. No one should take a box turtle where it is **illegal** to do so.

Some pet shops and reptile club members have box turtles for sale. Often pet shops will not sell animals that have been caught in the wild.

If you want a box turtle you should try to find one born in captivity.

GLOSSARY

captivity (kap TIV eh tee) — being kept by people in a cage, pen, or barn, not in the wild

carapace (KARE eh pis) — the upper, or top, part of a turtle's shell

habitat (HAB eh tat) — the type of place where an animal lives, such as a desert

hibernate (HY ber nayt) — to go into a deep, winter sleep

illegal (ih LEE gul) — against the law, unlawful

omnivore (OM nih vor) — an animal that eats both plant and animal foods

plastron (PLAS tren) — the under, or bottom, part of a turtle's shell

reptile (REP tyl) — that group of scaly, cold-blooded animals including snakes, turtles, lizards, the crocodile family, and the tuatara

INDEX

Further Reading

Patterson, Jordan. *Box Turtles: Keeping and Breeding Them in Captivity*.
    Chelsea House, 1998

Martin, Louise. *Turtles* Rourke Publishing, 1989

Websites To Visit

- www.wtgrain.org/turtle/w2needs.htm   • www.geocities.com/rainforest/vines/5504
- www.healthypet.com/library/nutrition-7.htm

About The Author

Lynn Stone is the author of over 400 children's books. He is a talented natural history photographer as well. Lynn, a former teacher, travels worldwide to photograph wildlife in their natural habitat.

DATE			